VETERANS DAY

by Brendan Flynn

Cody Koala

An Imprint of Pop!
popbooksonline.com

abdobooks.com

Published by Pop!, a division of ABDO, PO Box 398166, Minneapolis, Minnesota 55439. Copyright © 2019 by POP, LLC. International copyrights reserved in all countries. No part of this book may be reproduced in any form without written permission from the publisher. Pop!™ is a trademark and logo of POP, LLC.

Printed in the United States of America, North Mankato, Minnesota

092018
012019

THIS BOOK CONTAINS RECYCLED MATERIALS

Cover Photo: iStockphoto
Interior Photos: iStockphoto, 1, 5 (bottom left), 15, 19 (top), 19 (bottom left), 19 (bottom right), 20; Shutterstock Images, 5 (top), 5 (bottom right), 7, 9, 10, 12, 16, 17

Editor: Meg Gaertner
Series Designer: Laura Mitchell

Library of Congress Control Number: 2018949962

Publisher's Cataloging-in-Publication Data

Names: Flynn, Brendan, author.
Title: Veterans day / by Brendan Flynn.
Description: Minneapolis, Minnesota : Pop!, 2019 | Series: Holidays | Includes online resources and index.
Identifiers: ISBN 9781532162022 (lib. bdg.) | ISBN 9781641855730 (pbk) | ISBN 9781532163081 (ebook)
Subjects: LCSH: Veterans day--Juvenile literature. | Holidays--Juvenile literature. | National holidays--Juvenile literature.
Classification: DDC 394.264--dc23

Hello! My name is

Cody Koala

Pop open this book and you'll find QR codes like this one, loaded with information, so you can learn even more!

Scan this code* and others like it while you read, or visit the website below to make this book pop.

popbooksonline.com/veterans-day

*Scanning QR codes requires a web-enabled smart device with a QR code reader app and a camera.

Table of Contents

Chapter 1

Veterans Day

Flags are waving. A **retired** soldier gives a speech to a crowd. People cheer as a band plays. It is **Veterans** Day.

Watch a video here!

Veterans Day happens each year on November 11. It is a day to celebrate those who fought for our country.

Sometimes Veterans Day falls on a weekend. People celebrate it on the closest Friday or Monday instead.

November

Mon	Tue	Wed	Thu	Fri	Sat	Sun
						1
2	3	4	5	6	7	8
9	10	11	12	13	14	15
16	17	18	19	20	21	22
23	24	25	26	27	28	29
30						

Chapter 2

War Is Over

On November 11, 1918, World War I ended. The two sides signed an **armistice**. Many people had died in the war. Everyone was happy it was over.

Learn more here!

The **troops** came home from the war. Their friends and family celebrated. One year later, the whole country got a chance to **honor** them.

President Woodrow Wilson named November 11, 1919, as the first Armistice Day. It was a day to celebrate peace. It was also a day to show respect for the war veterans.

Chapter 3

Honoring Troops

In 1954 the government changed the holiday to Veterans Day. It would honor all veterans, not just those who fought in World War I.

Learn more here!

Many veterans are buried at Arlington National Cemetery. It is near Washington, DC.

The president gives

a speech there every

Veterans Day.

The Tomb of the Unknown Soldier remembers soldiers who died without being identified.

Chapter 4

Celebrations

Many schools and businesses are closed on Veterans Day. People celebrate with friends and family members who were in the **military**.

Complete an activity here!

People gather for parades. Some put flowers on the graves of their loved ones. They think about what veterans have done for the country.

Most government offices are closed on Veterans Day.

Making Connections

Text-to-Self

Are any of your family members veterans? How do you celebrate Veterans Day?

Text-to-Text

Have you read any other books about holidays? What did you learn?

Text-to-World

Veterans Day is a day to celebrate peace. In what ways do you see people sharing peace in the world?

Glossary

armistice – an agreement to stop fighting a war.

honor – to show respect.

military – the various groups of people who fight on behalf of a country.

retired – having left one's job.

troops – soldiers who fight in wars.

veteran – a person who has served in the military.

Index

Online Resources

popbooksonline.com

Thanks for reading this Cody Koala book!

Scan this code* and others like it in this book, or visit the website below to make this book pop!

popbooksonline.com/veterans-day

*Scanning QR codes requires a web-enabled smart device with a QR code reader app and a camera.